THE NOBLE ENGLISH ART OF SELF-DEFENCE

With Illustrations, Showing the Various Blows, Stops, and Guards

The London Library

Pushkin Press

Pushkin Press
71–75 Shelton Street
London WC2H 9JQ

Selection and editorial material © Pushkin Press and The London
Library 2016

Ned Donnelly, *Self-Defence; or, The Art of Boxing, with Illustrations
Showing the Various Blows, Stops, and Guards*. Edited by J. M. Waite.
London: Weldon & Co., 1879

"Ned Donnelly", published in *The National Sporting Club: Past and
Present*. Edited by A. F. Bettinson, and W. Outram Tristram. London:
Sands & Co., 1902

First published by Pushkin Press in 2016

9 8 7 6 5 4 3 2 1

ISBN 978 1 782273 19 6

Set in Goudy Modern by Tetragon, London

Printed by CPI Group (UK) Ltd, Croydon, CR0 4YY

www.pushkinpress.com

SELF-DEFENCE; OR, THE ART OF BOXING

BY NED DONNELLY

NED DONNELLY, a boxer and boxing instructor, was born in 1841. He was one of the most significant and successful instructors in the history of British boxing, noted for his "inborn knack of imparting his own knowledge". He was also fond of his drink, and a proficient step-dancer. He could not read or write, but among his pupils were King Edward VII and George Bernard Shaw. He died in 1911.

Ned Donnelly

Preface

In presenting to the public a book on the subject of the art which I pursue and profess, I think it necessary to explain, for the information of those who do not know me, the basis of my claim to their confidence as an authority on the noble English art of self-defence. He who would teach must first have learned; and in boxing a man learns best under the serious responsibility of actual encounters in the Prize Ring. A man who has boxed only with the gloves on, and has never had experience of a real fight, can be considered only as an amateur; though he may possibly be a good amateur. The boxer who may fairly claim to be a professional is the one who has practically encountered the dangers and the difficulties of fights with good antagonists. The Prize Ring is now extinct. The prizes have disappeared, but the lessons remain; and I may claim public confidence on the ground that a career commenced in the Ring has been successfully continued (and still continues) in the boxing school.

At the early age of seventeen my young enthusiasm for the fistic art had already led me to commence the study of boxing; but I did not actually taste the hardships, dangers, toils, and triumphs of the Ring until 1864, when, in my twentieth year, I was matched for the first time. I was trained carefully at Barnet, and in the month of January, 1864, I met in the roped ring and there defeated Styles, of Paddington. My first fight occupied sixteen and a half minutes, and was happily finished in ten rounds. My next opponent was Tom McKelvy, whom I fought and beat in July, 1866. In this fight I fought for an hour with my right arm disabled, in consequence of my antagonist falling upon me and putting out my shoulder. Only my left arm was left to me, and upon this single weapon I had to rely. Tom Sayers was reduced to a similar condition in the immortal fight with the giant Heenan. My second fight lasted one hour and twenty-one minutes, and was finished in twenty-one rounds. Both these encounters were arranged and brought off satisfactorily under the auspices of Nat Langham.

Since my retirement from the Prize Ring I have been and still am occupied in teaching boxing, and I may fairly boast of success with my pupils. I have, indeed, as I may modestly urge, been rather remarkably successful in teaching, since I have taught no less than fourteen winners of the Marquis of Queensberry's Cup. To use an old sporting phrase, "I am still to be heard of," at Mr. Waite's well-known school of arms, 22, Golden Square, Regent Street, where I give lessons, and where I may be seen any day between ten and six.

The Prize Ring may be dead, but boxing is still as much alive as ever, and must always form a part of the athletic education of every young Englishman. My experience both in fighting and in teaching has led me to believe that I could render service to students with the pen, as well as with the gloves on my hands;

hence this little manual of the noble art. If
any of my definitions with pencil or with pen
should seem to require further elucidation, I
shall be happy to demonstrate in person to any
pupil all and any of the glories of our art.

N. D.
22, Golden Square,
Regent Street, London, W.
1st January, 1879.

Self-Defence; or, The Art of Boxing

The Art of Boxing has been practised more or less among the two great nations of antiquity. The Greeks and Romans held it in high respect, and even the Jews did not wholly eschew the art of smiting, while the descendants of the Tribes who settled in England have contributed many of the most brilliant boxers to the roll of fame. That every man who desires the development of the muscular powers of the human frame, the possession of quickness, decision, endurance, and courage should practice boxing is a matter of necessity, since by no other means can all these qualities be so thoroughly tested and cultivated. Every man should be able to use the weapons which nature has given him to the best of his ability:——not necessarily to oppress or injure others (since the best boxers are almost invariably the least quarrelsome and overbearing persons), but to be able to defend himself from attack or oppression on the part of others. The smallest and weakest man, by assiduous practice in boxing, may make himself an antagonist by no means to be despised; and well do we remember seeing a small, pale, slender-looking slip of a fellow, give a great hulking waterman, six or eight inches taller than himself, a very wholesome thrashing at Hampton Court once for attempting to bully him out of his fare. It was beautiful to see how the little man slipped away under the arms of the big one (who was weaving and walloping them about like the sails of a windmill), propping him sharply here, there, and everywhere, until the bully, worn-out and bleeding, admitted that he had had enough, and the little one walked off without a mark, amid the cheers of the spectators. The big one was probably careful in future to deal more cautiously with

his customers. Boxing has been called brutal.
With persons who hold that view it is perhaps useless to argue; they look only at the
worst aspect of the *means*, and entirely shut
their eyes to the *object*, or better side of the
question. But it may fairly be asked whether
manners have improved since boxing was abol-
ished by law; whether there is less brutality,
less wife-beating and kicking, now than formerly; and whether the spectacle one so often
sees, of two great hulking brutes blackguard-
ing each other in the foulest and most filthy
language, yet both afraid to hit one another
from want of familiarity with the usages of
combat, is an improving one? Is there less brutality, less criminal violence, often attended
with fatal or nearly fatal results? less ready
use of un-English and unmanly weapons and
means of offence than there was formerly?
We say No, emphatically, and with certainty,
no. In the old days, when boxing flourished,
if a man had been seen ill-treating a weaker
one or beating and kicking a woman, twenty
men who could use their fists would have come

forward promptly "to help the weak," and the brute would soon have learnt at what a risk he indulged his propensities. Now twenty men will pass by on the other side, or scuttle off down a by-street to be out of the row.

Our great fatal mistake was made in putting down what was called "prize fighting." It was *first* declared illegal, and then tolerated for many years. The professors of the art being thus placed under a social ban, and having to practice it in opposition to the law, the more respectable and better class of their patrons became gradually weeded out, and while the Tom Springs and Deaf Burkes, men of sterling worth, courage, and unimpeachable honesty, passed away, worse came in their places; and then, this, the natural result of such a course of treatment was pointed to as a reason for active interference and putting fighting down altogether. Yet the native love of seeing a well *stricken* field was never so strongly displayed as when Tom Sayers and Heenan fought their well contested fight, and the best blood in England stood by the ring side and looked on with breathless interest. Had such patronage always awaited the ring, had endeavours been made to raise its status and social condition instead of lowering it; had it been recognised as a national benefit that the youth of England should know how to protect itself, should know how to bear exertion and pain with unflinching courage and endurance; had it been admitted that a school for the encouragement and practice of the art in which the highest efficiency could be obtained was a national requisite, then indeed we should have had matters placed on a different footing, and the rowdyism and blackguardism one used to hear so much of and which were mainly due to the low parasites and hangers on of the Ring would not have been heard of at all, for the professors of the art, seeing themselves respected, would have put all this down with a strong hand. As it is, the school of boxing is rapidly dying out, and when the professors of the present day have passed away it will be hard to say where the new ones are to come from. Unless, therefore, some strong step is taken to revive the fallen fortunes of the Ring, the school of British boxing will soon be a vision of the past, and Continental manners and practices of the worst type will find a home amongst us.

Useful Hints in Sparring

Keep your eyes open.

Abstain from biting your lips, or putting your tongue between your teeth. Very serious accidents may occur from so doing.

The mouth ought to be firmly closed. The slightest tap on the lower jaw when it is hanging loose will be remembered for long afterwards, while a more severe blow may dislocate it. The value of this piece of advice will be the more obvious to the reader if he attempts simply to shake his lower jaw when his mouth is closed and then repeat the experiment with it open.

Endeavour in sparring to let the muscles work as loosely and easily as possible. Let all your movements be light and free. Lift the feet, do not drag them. By these means you will cultivate quickness, without which, knowledge is of little use in boxing.

In sparring round your adversary keep the left hand and foot in front of you, and after delivering a blow, work to your right, in order to get out of reach of his right hand.

Wrestling is not permitted in boxing.

It is a foul blow to hit below the belt.

Avoid if possible coming to close quarters with a man of much superior weight. In out-fighting quickness may neutralize weight, but in in-fighting the latter must always tell.

It may perhaps be as well to explain the somewhat technical expressions of "in-fighting" and "out-fighting."

IN-FIGHTING means half-arm hitting, with both arms, when close to your antagonist. In in-fighting a man must rely upon his quickness in hitting and cannot pay much attention to guarding.

OUT-FIGHTING means long-arm hitting and guarding, and includes manoeuvring for a hit coupled with a readiness to guard.

Hitting

POSITION OF THE HANDS
AND ARMS, &c.

In hitting make as much use as possible of your weight. The blow that is simply delivered by the action of the muscles is nothing by comparison with that which is followed and driven home by the full weight of the body. Remember also to have the hands tightly closed. In fighting this would naturally be an unnecessary caution; it is, however, a frequent occurrence to see men hit with open gloves. Besides diminishing the force of the blow, a sprained or otherwise injured hand or wrist may follow.

In the left-hand lead off at the head, the blow should be given with the upper knuckles, and in all others with the hand in the position shown in plate XXXVII.

In leading off with the *left hand at the head* the arm should be perfectly straight, with the elbow turned under and palm upwards. *Vide* plate XXXVII.

For all other blows the arm should be slightly bent, the elbow pointing outwards and the palm turned half down and inwards. *Vide* plate XXXVII.

There are four hits, viz.:

The left hand at the head.

The left hand at the body.

The right hand at the head.

The right hand at the body.

Ducking

Ducking consists in throwing the head on one side and at the same time slightly lowering the body, so as to allow the blow intended for the head to pass harmlessly over the shoulder. It is an excellent method of avoiding a blow, affording, moreover, an opportunity of delivering one, for the pupil should bear in mind never to duck without at the same time hitting. When opposed to a bigger man than yourself, fight at his body, using the ducks shown in plates X. and XIII.

There are five ducks:

The duck to the right, as practised when countering with the left hand on the head. *Vide* plate XIX.

The duck to the right, when it is intended to deliver a left-hand body blow. *Vide* plate X.

The duck to the left while delivering a right-hand cross-counter. *Vide* plate XX.

The duck to the left, giving at the same time a right-hand body blow. *Vide* plate XIII.

The duck to the right, which is sometimes used when leading off at the head with the left hand, in order to avoid a counter. *Vide* plate IX.

Feinting

A feint is a false attack made to divert attention from the real danger which follows, as, for instance, a left-hand feint followed by a right-hand blow, or a feint at the head followed by a body blow. To make a feint with the left hand, straighten the arm suddenly as though you were going to deliver a blow, and at the same time advance the left foot about six inches, keeping the head back, then return to the guard.

A feint with the right hand is made thus: draw the arm back suddenly as though you were going to hit, and at the same time advance the left foot about six inches, keeping the head back, then return to the guard. "Drawing" has some affinity with feinting, and may be described under the same head. Its object is to induce your opponent to deliver a certain blow for which you are prepared, and which it is your intention to counter; you do this either by feinting and enticing him to follow you up, or by laying yourself open with apparent carelessness to the attack you wish him to make. Both are, of course, exceedingly useful, but the beginner will do well to cultivate quickness and attain some proficiency in straightforward sparring before he turns his attention to manoeuvres which are more likely to get himself than his adversary into trouble if they are not performed with great rapidity. When your opponent feints or attempts to draw you, either get back or else guard both head and body as illustrated in plate VII.

A Left Hand Feint and Lead Off

Feint a lead off with the left hand, so as to induce your adversary to throw up his right-hand guard. Should he do so, hit at the pit of the stomach. Should he not raise his right hand, follow the feint up with a genuine lead off at the head. Particular attention should be paid in this attack to the action of the feet. Make a short step with the left foot (about six inches) as though you were going to lead off, then withdraw it and suddenly deliver the blow; using the feet as described in plates VI. and X. This movement requires some practice, as it should be performed with great rapidity.

PLATE I

Attitude

In this position the toes of the right foot must be directly behind and in a line with the left heel. The distance between the feet naturally varies according to the height; for a man of 5ft. 8in. it should be 14 inches. Let the right foot be turned slightly out, and raise the heel about two inches from the ground; the weight then will rest on the ball of the foot. The left foot ought to be flat on the ground and pointed towards your opponent's left toe. Slightly bend

23

both knees. The right arm should be across the "mark" (that point where the ribs begin to arch), the hand being an inch below the left breast. To obtain the exact position of the left arm, advance the left shoulder, drop the arm by the side, and then raise the fore-arm until the hand is on a level with the elbow. In sparring it should be worked easily forward and backward. Throw the right shoulder well back, and slightly sink it, so that of the two the left shoulder is the higher. Lower the chin, turn the face a little to the right, and bend the head slightly over the right shoulder. The object of turning the face is to prevent both eyes being hit at once, while the head is bent to the right in order that it may not be directly in a line with your opponent's left hand, and thus afford him an easy target.

The Double Lead Off at Body and Head

Commence with the body blow as described in No. X.; instead, though, of retiring immediately you have struck out, bring the right foot about twelve inches forward, step in a few inches with the left, and follow the first blow up with a second aimed at the face. Both blows, which must follow one another as rapidly as possible, should be delivered with the left hand. The palm in each instance ought to be turned down.

PLATE II

Shaking Hands

Both before and after a bout with the gloves, the combatants should thus salute one another. It is a good old fashioned English custom, betokening friendly feeling and should never be omitted. A hearty shake of the hands after a warm set-to, in which both men have perhaps become rather more earnest than is necessary, at once dissipates what might otherwise grow into ill feeling. As the hand is extended, move the right foot to the front, and at the

conclusion of the ceremony throw it smartly
behind the left and assume at once the position
given in plate I.

PLATE III

Both Men on Guard

It is of the utmost importance that a man should stand and get about well. The advantage of quick hands is sadly neutralized by slow legs. To get about quickly and safely, there must be some arrangement and method in the steps. An experienced boxer, who has paid attention to the action of the feet, always stands firmly; his feet are never flurried, the same distance usually separates them; he moves rapidly, neatly, and quietly. With a novice, or boxer who imagines that getting about is an unimportant detail, and the manner in which he moves of no consequence, the case is different. As a rule his movements are few and deplorably slow; when suddenly attacked, he loses his balance, and most of his attention is consequently directed to saving himself from falling. Should he, however, be more ambitious, and attempt to move with any rapidity, the whole performance is a scramble. His feet are too close together, or too far apart, his legs are (if I may use such an expression) constantly in his way; he stumbles, staggers, and rolls about in an absurd manner, not unfrequently ending by tripping himself up, and falling even without the assistance of a blow.

By referring to the plate you will see both men on guard, in the position illustrated in plate No. I., and before proceeding further they should practice the following steps:—

To advance, move the left foot about ten inches forward, placing it upon the ground heel first. Let the right foot follow it the same distance. Bear in mind that the space between the feet should vary as little as possible.

To retire, step back about ten inches with the right foot, following it in like manner with the left.

To take ground to the right, move the left foot about twelve inches to the right, following it immediately with the right, and assuming again position No. I.

To take ground to the left, move the right foot twelve inches to the left, and place the left directly in front of it.

By adopting these steps the right foot is always behind the left, you are always in position, and consequently ready either for attack or defence.

PLATE IV

Breaking Ground

This is the term applied to the usual method of retreat in boxing. You break ground in the following manner. In leading off at the head your right foot will be raised from the ground (*vide* plate VII.). As you set it down again and the weight of the body is transferred to it from the left leg, spring backwards. The left foot should touch the ground first, alighting on the same spot upon which you formerly placed the right, which then assumes its natural position in the rear. You will thus find yourself in position a pace behind the spot from which you originally stepped in to lead off. It is necessary sometimes, if your opponent follows you up very quickly, to double the step, that is to say, to make two consecutive springs backwards. For other blows, although the right foot is not raised from the ground at the moment of striking, the movements in breaking ground are precisely the same, for the moment the weight falls on the right leg you spring back as described above.

Guard for Lead Off at the Head with the Right

Raise the left elbow and bend the arm so that the fist is somewhat lower and nearer to the body than the elbow. Let the palm be turned to the front. Shift the right foot back about six inches, and lean a little forward, so that you are the better able to resist the attack. Look over your wrist, and receive the blow upon the elbow.

PLATE V

Side Step

This is exceedingly useful in avoiding a rush or in getting away when you are driven back against the ropes. We will suppose you to be in position facing your adversary. By a sudden movement of the feet, half spring half step, you turn the body to the right, change the relative position of the legs, and assume the attitude of a fencer on the lunge, that is with the right instead of left leg in front, as is usual in boxing. Your left should now be turned towards your adversary, the line of your feet being at right angles to the line in which they formerly stood. The left foot should be upon almost the same spot formerly occupied by your right. If your adversary advances hastily and without caution whilst you are in this posture he will be apt to trip over your left leg. Bring the left foot into position before the right, and you will then stand a pace to the right of your original station. If this step is executed rapidly you elude your opponent, for he will no longer be in front of you, and consequently you can easily get away from the ropes. A combination of the side step and breaking ground should also be practised. Spring back as if breaking ground, and alight in the posture above described as that of a fencer on the lunge, with the body turned to the right, bring the left foot into position before the right, and you thus get back and work to the right of yourself at the same time.

Left-Hand Counter on the Body

This should be delivered when your adversary is leading off at your head with his left hand.

Duck to the right, step in about twelve inches, and aim your blow at the pit of his stomach. The right hand should be drawn seven or eight inches back, and held close to the side. To get away, turn the left heel out and spring well back. Do not raise the head until out of distance.

PLATE VI

Left-Hand Lead Off at the Head Without Guarding

The lead off at the head should, as a rule, be made with the left hand. Its importance can hardly be exaggerated. Every effort should therefore be directed towards attaining proficiency in this particular. A quick lead off frequently enables a man to score point after point without receiving a return. He spars round his adversary, watching for an opportunity, and then having measured his distance well, steps in, plants a blow, and is away again at once. With these tactics at his command, a light man will often fight a heavy weight all over without coming to close quarters, at which weight would inevitably tell in favour of its possessor. A slow lead off lays a man open to counters and cross-counters, which will hereafter be described.

The lead off should be made when the hand is in the position shown in plate No. I. In all other blows the hand is more or less drawn back before delivery; in this case, however, it should come straight out, as it were, spontaneously, and without the slightest hesitation. Beginners are almost always inclined to hit downwards, or "chop" and bear heavily upon their opponent's guard. This should be avoided. In stepping in push yourself off the ball of the right foot, and spring in about eighteen inches. The action of foot and arm should be simultaneous; do not step in and then deliver the blow. The load off at the head with the left hand is the only blow that is delivered while the right foot is raised from the ground.

As you step in the right foot should follow, and at the moment of striking, hang over the spot formerly occupied by the left. Full advantage is thus taken of height and reach. Be careful when you step in to place the left foot upon the ground, heel first. If the toe touches the ground first, and your adversary by chance gets back instead of guarding or receiving your blow, you do not meet with the expected resistance, and consequently are apt to over-balance; in which case, until you can recover yourself, you are at his mercy. The head and right hand remain in position No. I.

PLATE VII

Right-Hand Guard for the Head

To guard the head from your opponent's left
hand, raise the right hand nearly to a level and
in front of the left temple. Let the fore-arm
cross the face, and be thrown forward so as
to turn instead of receiving the weight of the
blow. Keep the elbow down. Close the hand
firmly in order to brace the sinews, and turn
the palm partly outward or the blow will fall
on the bone of the arm instead of the muscle.
At the same time bend the head forward and

to the right—thus, although the face is well out of danger, you can still see your opponent over the fore-arm.

PLATE VIII

Left-Hand Lead Off at Head and Guard

The lead off in this case is precisely the same, but, at the moment of hitting, you also throw up the right hand guard to protect the face from a possible left hand counter. It requires a little practice to do this without detracting from the rapidity of your lead off; your trouble will however be well spent, for with an opponent who frequently attempts left-hand counters this will be found a very useful manoeuvre. *For* the feint for this lead off, *see* p. 22.

PLATE IX

Left-Hand Lead Off and Duck

This illustration represents the same lead off
again. In place of the right-hand guard, it
is, however, accompanied with a duck, thus
avoiding instead of guarding the left-hand
counter. Observe that for this blow the right
foot is not raised; it does not follow the left as
in the preceding examples, but remains firmly
planted on the ground, as in the left-hand body
blow.

PLATE X

Left-Hand Body Blow

This blow should never be attempted unless
you are confident that you have sufficient
room behind you to be able to get well away
again. It should be directed at the pit of the
stomach, which is the weakest part of the
body. Occasionally it may with advantage be
preceded by a feint at the head, in order to
induce your opponent to throw up his right
hand guard and lay the "mark" open. Let
the ball of the right foot be kept well on the

ground. Step in about thirty inches with the left foot, hitting out at the same time and ducking to the right. In the event of your adversary attempting to counter you with the left, your head will thus be outside his arm, which will pass harmlessly over your left shoulder. For this blow the arm should be slightly bent, the elbow turned out, and the palm of the hand turned inwards and partly down. The right arm should in the meantime be drawn back seven or eight inches, and the glove held close to the side. To get away, turn the left heel outwards and spring well back, taking care not to raise the head until out of distance.

PLATE XI

Stop for Left-Hand Body Blow

Like all stops this requires very accurate timing. Having foreseen your adversary's intention, hit him full in the face with your left hand before he can get his head down. Keep your right arm in its original position across the "mark."

PLATE XII

Guard for Left-Hand Body Blow

It is customary, in order to prevent the preceding "double," to cover both body and head at the same time. When, therefore, the body is attacked put up the right hand guard, and at the same time throw the left arm well across the "mark" (*vide* plate VII.). Be careful to hold it firmly against the body, for even the jar of a severe body blow will knock a good deal of the wind out of a man. Step back about six inches with the right foot, so as to be the better able to resist a rush.

This is also a guard for double lead off at body and head described on p. 25.

PLATE XIII

Right-Hand Body Blow

This should be aimed at a little below the heart.
It is delivered under the same circumstances
and in the same manner as the left-hand body
blow (*vide* No. X.), with these exceptions:
you duck to the left instead of right, and the
feet when you have stepped in should only be
twenty inches apart instead of thirty; you
have consequently to get nearer your opponent
before attempting it. Be sure always that you
have sufficient room behind you for retreat.

Should he attempt to put his left arm round your neck while you are delivering this blow, duck to your right under his arm and get away. This should always be done when a man attempts to seize your head. When opposed to a man who stands with the right leg in front, you must duck to your left.

PLATE XIV

Stop for Right-Hand Body Blow

This stop is exactly the same as that recom-
mended for the left-hand body blow. *Vide*
No. XI.

PLATE XV

Guard for Right-Hand Body Blow

Bring the left side forward and drop the left arm, which should be slightly bent, so as to cover the side and front of the thigh. Care should be taken to press the arm close to the body, in order to prevent the jar through which you would otherwise feel much of the force of the blow.

PLATE XVI

A Lead Off at the Head with the Right, and Guard for it

Feint with the left, hitting your opponent on the right arm. Do not withdraw your hand, but as he raises his guard rest upon it with your left and pin it to his chest; then bring in the right hand, aiming it at the chin or angle of the jaw. Properly delivered this is a most punishing blow, for by steadying yourself with the left hand you can bring your full force into play with the right. *For* guard for lead off at the head with the right, *see* p. 32.

PLATE XVII

Lead Off with Right Hand at Head, and Duck

When leading off at the head with the right, you may duck to the left, and avoid a right-hand counter. In this illustration both men are performing this manoeuvre.

PLATE XVIII

Left-Hand Counter on the Head

This happens when two men lead off at the head with the left hand at the same time.

PLATE XIX

Left-Hand Counter on the Head, and Duck

There are perhaps few blows more unpleasantly startling than a good left-hand counter which meets you full-face. It opens a spacious firmament to the bewildered eyes, wherein you discover more new planets in a second than the most distinguished astronomer ever observed in a lifetime. As your adversary leads off at your head with his left hand, duck to the right so as to allow his blow to pass over

55

your left shoulder; step in about twelve inches and strike out at his face. The right foot should not be moved. Here both men have, as it happens, made use of the same stratagem; in consequence of which, both left arms have passed harmlessly over each other's left shoulder.

Left-Hand Counter on the Head, and Guard

The difference between this and the preceding counter will be easily understood by studying the plate. It consists simply in guarding your opponent's lead off instead of ducking to avoid it. You step in and hit out as before.

PLATE XX

Right-Hand Cross Counter

This is the most severe blow which can be dealt in sparring. It is delivered as follows:—As your opponent leads off at your head with his left hand, step in about twelve inches, ducking to the left, at the same time shooting your right hand across his left arm and shoulder. The blow should be aimed either at the angle of the jaw or chin, and the palm of the hand should be half turned down. Let both feet be turned slightly to the left, as by these means the right side is brought forward and greater force given to the blow. As the counter is delivered, draw the left hand back to the position illustrated in the plate, then, should a second blow be necessary, before getting away you can deliver it.

PLATE XXI

Stop for Right-Hand
Cross Counter

Anticipating your adversary's intention, hit him full in the face with the left hand before he ducks; or, instead of striking at his face, deliver the blow on the right side of his chest near to the shoulder, and his right hand will be effectually stopped.

Another Stop for Right-Hand Cross Counter

As you lead off with your left drop the head well forward, so that at the end of the movement your left ear will be touching the inside of your upper arm when the angle of your jaw and chin will be completely covered by your shoulder.

Body blows with left or right hand will act as stops for all right hand hits at the head.

For left-hand counter on the body, *see* p. 35.

PLATE XXII

Right-Hand Counter

This occurs when both men lead off together
with the right hand.

PLATE XXIII

Stop for Right-Hand Counter

Duck your head to the left as you lead off.

Right-Hand Counter on the Body

Duck to the left in order to avoid your opponent's lead off, and strike out with the right
hand at a point a little below the heart. The
left hand should be drawn back as shown in
the illustration. In all other particulars this
blow represents the preceding. For this and

the left-hand counter, it will be well to study the right and left hand body blows (Nos. XIII. and X.), for, with the exception of the circumstances under which they are delivered, and the difference in the distance of the advance made, the blows are the same.

PLATE XXIV

Left-Hand Upper Cut

This blow, which in reality is a counter, should
be given when a man in leading off at your
head with his left hand holds his head down.
Guard your face with the right arm, step in
about twelve inches, and hit upwards with the
left. The arm should be bent and elbow turned
down. The force of the blow must come in a
great measure from the body.

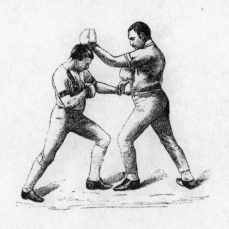

PLATE XXV

Draw and Stop for Left-
Hand Upper Cut

Feint a lead off at your opponent's face with
your head down, then duck to the right, and
give the left-hand body blow as described in
No. X.

PLATE XXVI

Right-Hand Upper Cut

With this exception that you do not guard, this
blow is similar to and delivered under the same
circumstances as the left-hand upper cut. In
delivering it the head should be slightly bent
to the left.

PLATE XXVII

A Draw and Stop for
Right-Hand Upper Cut

Feint with the head as if it were your intention to lead off with it down, then throw the
head back and lead off at your adversary's face
with the left hand.

PLATE XXVIII

Another Draw and Stop for Right-Hand Upper Cut

Feint a lead off at your opponent's face with your left hand, then duck to the left and put in the right-hand body blow. The reader should notice in this, as in other illustrations, the position of the hand not absolutely in use. Never drop your hands until out of distance.

PLATE XXIX

How to Prevent Your Antagonist
from Hitting After You
Have Led Off and Passed
Over His Left Shoulder

When this occurs, bend the elbow quickly, place your fore-arm against his throat, and thrust his head back. Grasp his left shoulder with your left hand and seize his left elbow with your right hand. This will effectually stop him from hitting you.

PLATE XXX

Slipping

This is an exceedingly useful manoeuvre,
which enables you to avoid a rush or get out
of a corner. Feint a lead off, tapping your
adversary lightly on the chest or right arm; do
not then retire, but as he comes at you duck
to the right, make another step forward (as
described in the lead off with a double step
in), and pass under his left arm. To face him
again turn to the left.

PLATE XXXI

The Head in Chancery

No directions can be given for getting a man into this position. When in close quarters you should, however, always be on the look out for a chance of doing so. If it occurs, grasp your opponent firmly round the neck with the left arm and use the right to punish him.

PLATE XXXII

To Get Out of Chancery

Almost the best advice to give a man who is firmly and fairly caught in chancery is not to attempt to get out, at least unless the hold loosens, and he can make his effort with some chance of success. In pulling away or resisting he is simply hanging himself. He should, therefore, push his opponent back (see plate XXXI.), and at the same time fight to the best of his ability with both hands. If, however, he discovers the danger before the grasp has tightened, he should place one hand under his adversary's fore-arm near the elbow, the other under the shoulder, and push the arm up, ducking at the same time, and dragging the head away.

PLATE XXXIII

In-Fighting

In-fighting generally takes place in a corner or near the side of the ring. In in-fighting bring the right foot forward until it is nearly in a line with the left, drop the chin and lean forward so as to receive the blows on the forehead. Keep your eyes fixed on your antagonist. Use both hands and hit rapidly, bringing the shoulder well forward at each blow. The arms should not be drawn too far back, as time is lost thereby; a great deal of the force of the blow is obtained by turning the body slightly to right or left as you hit. It is a great advantage to have your hands inside your opponent's, you should therefore keep them as close together as possible, so as to obtain, or if you already have it, keep this advantage. Aim the left hand at the eyes and nose, the right at the chin or angle of the jaw. After delivering five or six blows, get away. Never fight at the body in in-fighting, invariably make the head your mark.

PLATE XXXIV

Two Men on Guard, One with Left and the Other with Right Leg in Front

PLATE XXXV

*Guard for Right-Hand Lead
Off at Head When Opposed
to a Man Who Stands with
Right Leg in Front*

PLATE XXXVI

*Duck and Counter for a Lead
Off at Head by a Man Who
Stands with Right Leg in Front*

The Way to Deal with a Man Who Stands with His Right Leg and Right Arm in Front

Work to your left in order to avoid his left hand. Be chary in leading off with the left hand, as that is at once difficult and dangerous. It is far better to lead off with the right hand and duck at the same time to the left. When your adversary leads off with the right hand, duck to the left and counter either upon the face or body.

The blow on the face must be given like the right cross counter (*vide* plate XX.) and the one on the body like the right-hand body blow shown in plate XIII., except that you must aim at the pit of the stomach instead of at a little below the heart.

The Guards for an Opponent Who Stands with His Right Leg in Front

When he leads off with the right-hand guard with the left arm as shown in plate XXXV., guard his left with your right arm, as shown in plate VII.

Use the guards illustrated in plates XV. and XII. for his right and left hand body blows, guarding his right with your left and his left with your right.

Avoid in-fighting with him as much as possible.

I have now, to the best of my ability, described the principal hits, stops, guards, &c., in boxing, as I use and teach them myself. Having to a certain extent perfected himself in these, the pupil will do well to go through the following exercises, making the hits as smartly and as rapidly in succession as possible, but not omitting to return to the position illustrated in plate No. I. after each blow. The opponents should take it in turns to guard and attack.

1st Exercise

1.—Left-hand body blow (get back).
2.—Right-hand body blow (get back).
3.—Left-hand lead off at the head, guarding with the right (get back).
4.—Right-hand cross counter (get back).
5.—Lead off at the head with the left and duck to the right (get back).

2nd Exercise

1.—Right-hand body blow (get back).
2.—Lead off with the left at the head without guarding (get back).
3.—Right-hand cross counter (get back).
4.—Left-hand body blow (get back).
5.—Lead off with the left at the head and duck (get back).

3rd Exercise

1.—Lead off with the left hand at the head without guarding (get back).
2.—Right-hand cross counter (get back).
3.—Left-hand lead off at the head and duck to the right (get back).
4.—Left-hand body blow (get back).
5.—Right-hand body blow (get back).

4th Exercise

1.—Lead off with left at body, then make a short step in and repeat the blow on the face (get back). (*This is the double lead off at body and head,* vide *page* 25.)
2.—Lead off with left and right at head (get back).
3.—As your opponent retires, advance quickly, then step in and deliver the left on the face (get back).
4.—Both men lead off with left and guard (get back).

5th Exercise

1.—Lead off with the left hand at the head (get back).
2.—Right-hand cross counter, remain and commence in-fighting, deliver five or six blows and get back.

Never degenerate into a rough, unmeaning, unscientific scramble. In the midst of impetuosity remember coolness; and never let the heat of action lead you to forget good-temper. Be manly; seek no undue advantage. Science and pluck give advantage enough.

PLATE XXXVII

Positions of the Hands When Hitting

LEFT-HAND LEAD OFF AT HEAD

RIGHT-HAND CROSS COUNTER

LEFT-HAND BODY BLOW

RIGHT-HAND BODY BLOW

Boxing Competitions

There is no published code of rules for the management of boxing competitions or for the guidance of the judges, so I beg to offer the following suggestions, which may be of service until a proper set has been formed by some recognised authority.

In boxing competitions, there should be four judges, a referee, and timekeeper; a judge to sit at each corner of the ring (outside), and the referee to move about so that he may see the whole of the manoeuvring and hitting, and at the end of each round the referee and judges should assemble and decide, during the interval between the rounds, which man has had the advantage. When the judges sit together, they cannot possibly see all the hits given.

The competitors should toss for corners.

The referee should under no circumstances be the timekeeper, as he cannot both keep time and watch the rounds.

In judging, both body and head blows, indeed, all the points in boxing should be taken into consideration, as well as form and style.

In-fighting should not be ignored and looked upon as roughing. There is great art in it, and in a street fight it is much more useful than out-fighting.

The competitors should be divided into four weights, termed "Feather," "Light," "Middle," and "Heavy," viz:—

Feather for men under 8 stone.

Light for men under 10 stone.

Middle for men under 11 st. 4 lbs.

Heavy for men of any weight.

Three rounds should be sparred, the first and second of three minutes duration each, and the third of four minutes. A minute allowed between the rounds.

On time being called, the men should go into the middle of the ring and begin the round and continue it, unless an accident should happen, until the judges stop them.

No wrestling, kicking, hitting below the mark, butting, striking with the elbow or palm, or taking hold of the hair should be permitted; any man wilfully doing any of the above, should be first cautioned and, upon a repetition, disqualified by the judges.

In striking, the blow *must* be delivered with the hand closed.

The seconds should not be allowed to be in the ring, except during intervals between the rounds, neither should they be permitted to direct their men during a round, either by word or sign.

When a competitor draws a bye, he should invariably be compelled to spar three rounds of the same duration as the others.

No competitor should be allowed to lay hold of the ropes to assist him in the contest.

Any competitor who may be disabled during a round, and not be able to renew the contest before sixty seconds have expired, shall be considered beaten.

How to Pitch a Ring

The ground should be level, and where there is sufficient room the ring should be 24 feet square, formed of two lines of ropes and eight stakes.

The stakes should be strong, with round tops, and have holes or rings through which to run the ropes, and should be firmly fixed in the ground, out of which they should stand 5 feet.

Two rows of ropes of 4 inches in circumference should be run round the ring, the bottom one about 2 feet 3 inches from the ground, and the top one 4 feet 3 inches.

When the ring is on a raised stage, a stout piece of wood about 5 or 6 inches deep should be fixed all round the edge of the floor to prevent the men slipping off.

Under no circumstances should the ring be less than 12 feet square. In a ring of less dimensions the men would not have sufficient room to use their feet, without which there can be no good boxing.

Winners of the Marquis of Queensberry's Boxing Championship Cups Since the Commencement of the Competitions

HEAVY WEIGHTS

1867	J. C. Halliday	1873	F. B. Maddison
1868	T. Milvain	1874	D. Gibson
1869	No competition	1875	A. L. Highton
1870	H. J. Chinnery	1876	R. Wakefield
1871	H. J. Chinnery	1877	J. M. R. Francis
1872	E. B. Michell	1878	R. Frost Smith

MIDDLE WEIGHTS

1867	H. J. Chinnery	1873	A. Walker
1868	H. J. Chinnery	1874	F. R. Thomas
1869	H. J. Chinnery	1875	J. H. Douglas
1870	E. B. Michell	1876	J. H. Douglas
1871	E. C. Streatfield	1877	J. H. Douglas
1872	H. J. Blyth	1878	G. I. Garland

LIGHT WEIGHTS

1867	R. Cleminson	1873	C. T. Hobbs
1868	No competition	1874	L. Dénéréaz
1869	H. L. Jeyes, W. O.	1875	H. S. Giles
1870	R. V. Churton	1876	A. Bultitude
1871	R. V. Churton	1877	H. Skeate
1872	R. V. Churton	1878	G. Airey

Pushkin Press—The London Library

"Found on the Shelves"

THE LONDON LIBRARY (a registered charity) is one of the UK's leading literary institutions and a favourite haunt of authors, researchers and keen readers.

Membership is open to all.

Join at www.londonlibrary.co.uk.

www.pushkinpress.com